# A Biography of Johnny Sexton

*The Story of One of the Greatest Irish Rugby Legend and Players of All Time*

GW00455038

**JONATHAN JOHNSON**

# TABLE OF CONTENTS

# Introduction

Johnny Sexton, a standout for Ireland, has disclosed that he has been gaining job experience as he gets ready for life beyond rugby later this year.

The seasoned fly-half, who will retire after the Rugby World Cup in 2023, stated in an interview that he most likely won't enter the coaching field.

"I wouldn't say never, because you never know what life is going to throw at you," Sexton said.

Even if an opportunity came through, I wouldn't be immediately interested in coaching players I've recently played with.

"I would never want to ruin this year because the relationship changes quickly if they find out you are mentoring them. I'm not going to do it right now.

"Rugby is my passion and everything I've ever known. I've been doing it for at least 20 years—possibly longer when I was younger. But I believe it's crucial to leave it behind and attempt something new. We'll then wait and see what occurs.

I've been doing some work experience there for the past few years, one day a week, so I'll go into that and see how it goes. "I'll go and see if I can do something in the business sector.

Possibly not for me. I might immediately get the itch and leave retirement to play for St. Marys!"

The famed Irish rugby captain Johnny Sexton's management company saw a huge increase in collected profits over the previous year. Profits increased by about £307,000, reaching a remarkable total of almost £2.5 million.

# Chapter 1: Early Life

## Sexton's childhood in Dublin

Jonathan Sexton was born in Dublin, Ireland, on the eleventh day of July 1985 to parents Clare Sexton and Jerry Sexton. He is the first child of his gorgeous parents, who also have a daughter and three sons.

Johnny came from a sporting family. For the 1881-founded Bective Rangers rugby union team in Dublin, Ireland, his father was an active rugby union player.

Little Johnny took to the game naturally since he was close to his father. His father, Jerry, first took him to a rugby game at Lansdowne Road when he was six years old. In his own words: "I can remember being carried by my father to the opening game on Lansdowne Road. We simply made the descent from Donnybrook.

One of his oldest and fondest childhood memories still endures.

Johnny, who was sporting a tiny Ireland jersey, fell in love with sports right away. He had no idea that he would go down in history as one of his country's finest out-half.

## His Education

One of Jerry, Johnny's father's main concerns, was considering retirement. He wished to continue to live his dream through his kid, Johnny, to deal with it and prevent it from having an impact on his mind.

While Johnny was a student at St. Mary's College RFC, he learned a lot from his father. The rugby sensation's first experience was with Bective Rangers.

Jerry Sexton, Johnny Sexton's father, had given him a keen eye for a ball. He also possessed the brute strength that his uncle Willie, a former Irish Rugby player, was known for.

## His early introduction to Rugby

He realized early on that he was destined for stardom. Due to his dedication to the sport, St Mary's College Football Club, a rugby union team headquartered in South Dublin, Ireland, hired Johnny. Due to his dependability and indestructibility, Sexton quickly cemented his position in Irish rugby mythology.

## Chapter 2: Club Career

### Sexton's early days with Leinster

He scored the game-winning drop goal in the 2002 Leinster schools final at a drenched and muddy Lansdowne Road, which was a turning point in his early career.

Johnny was chosen for Leinster, one of Ireland's four professional provincial rugby teams, as a result of his work at St. Mary's.

In 2005, Johnny Sexton joined Leinster after having a fruitful career at the club and school levels.

He made his provincial debut in the 2005–06 campaign as a replacement against the Border Reivers.

Early on at Leinster, Sexton had a difficult time. For the number 10 jersey, he had to outplay more seasoned players Felipe Contepomi and David Holwell. In addition, he had to become adjusted to the demands of professional rugby, which were far higher than those of club and school rugby.

Despite the difficulties, Sexton displayed flashes of genius during his early Leinster career. In the last seconds of Leinster's thrilling triumph over Leicester Tigers in the quarterfinal of the 2006–07 Heineken Cup, he scored a drop goal. He was also crucial to Leinster's Pro12 championship triumph in 2008.

2009 marked Sexton's breakthrough season. Sexton had the chance to establish himself as the province's top fly-half because Contepomi had departed Leinster to join Stade Français. He made the most of the chance and assisted Leinster in winning the Heineken Cup for the second time in three years.

In addition, he received the Heineken Cup Player of the Year award for his efforts during the campaign that year.

Johnny started competing for the British and Irish Lions national team in 2013, which was seen as a contentious decision.

He also made another contentious switch to Racing 92 in that year to secure a £540,000-a-year contract, which caused some supporters to believe he was lured by celebrity.

When Johnny Sexton revealed in September of that same year that he had signed a deal to bring him back to

Leinster, there was another round of strong transfer rumors throughout the summer of 2014.

Sexton has now gone on to become one of Leinster's all-time greatest players. With the province, he has won four Heineken Cups, five Pro12 championships, and three European Rugby Champions Cups. He has received multiple individual honors, including World Rugby Player of the Year in 2018. He is also Ireland's most-capped player.

Early on in his time with Leinster, Sexton faced difficulties, but he overcame them with incredible tenacity and resilience. Since then, he has developed into one of the best players in the province's history.

After Keith Wood in 2001, Johnny Sexton became just the second Irish player in history to get the honor.

Jonathan Sexton is still regarded as one of the best fly halves in the world because of his exquisitely sophisticated blend of precision and force. The rest, as they say, is now history.

# Chapter 3: International Career

## Sexton's debut for Ireland

Johnny Sexton's competitive nature was present from the beginning of his Irish career.

Alternatively, the false start.

At the comparatively late age of 24, Sexton earned his Test debut against Fiji in November 2009. The Dubliner recalled why he was "gutted" in the lead-up to his 100th cap on Saturday.

"I recall Paddy Wallace suffering a blood injury the week before I was on the bench for the Australia match, and I took off the kit as quickly as I could to attempt to go on the field," Sexton remembered.

I was on the field at Croke Park when Paddy jumped back up, put on his helmet, and continued playing. I was devastated.

"The fact that I missed the first few days of that week crushed my heart. But the Fiji game will always be remembered for how miserable the weather was.

I was on the field at Croke Park when Paddy jumped back up, put on his helmet, and continued playing. I was devastated.

"I'll always remember waiting in line for the national anthem. It's strange getting your first cap in the RDS, but I remember thinking as I was getting in line, 'What did I do to deserve getting my first cap in this weather?'"

"But happily, we delivered a strong showing and a solid victory.

The following week I played South Africa in a major game, and you could tell the difference in a Test week like that.

"People in the room stood out to you as distinctive. That was perhaps my first experience playing Test rugby because of the different approach.

To describe how he works to stay in front of the pack for club and country, Sexton draws on his time playing for Leinster.

Until Joey Carbery, who is also in the Ireland squad for the November internationals, regains his best form, another out-half emerges from the pack, or Harry Byrne, who is also in the squad, can challenge him, he is still Andy Farrell's first choice at no. 10.

"Sexton reasoned, "There's no point in contemplating what will happen if this person starts ripping it up.

Nothing you can do will change that. It's about taking control of what you can and letting go of other people's actions.

"When Isa Nacewa was signed by Leinster early in my career, I had already learned a valuable lesson.

He was most likely signed as a 10, and Michael Cheika was always harping on about how brilliantly Isa attacked the line and accomplished various tasks.

He was always playing 10, so I began to imitate him, but I wasn't doing what I normally do. I lost my form at the beginning of the year because of that.

"I was attempting to convince him that I could play on par with Felipe or Isa. I have to utilize my advantages.

"I believe that carried over to me. You must exercise control over your strengths and strive to use them on the field.

Sexton said he would defer to others to discuss his contributions to the game and that he felt "lucky" and "privileged" to have the kind of career that his brother Mark wasn't able to have because of an injury.

The World Player of the Year for 2018 acknowledges that it has thrilled him that he has been able to recover from both his highs and lows and that he hopes to participate in the 2023 World Cup in France at the age of 38.

The Leinster talisman observed, "Durable wouldn't be a word that's been used to describe me too often, but it's day to day."

I received daily instruction from the men who came before me, including Paul O'Connell, Brian O'Driscolls, and Isa Nacewas.

"Even when they weren't working out, they were in the studio making movies, doing additional work, making sure they were getting enough rest, and going through the necessary motions in the gym.

It's day-to-day, then. That is the stuff that adds up. Joe Schmidt has, in my opinion, always insisted that you must lead by example rather than by telling the leadership group what to do.

"Hopefully that's still the case."

Sexton expressed sadness for missing two particular games: the 2015 finals game between Argentina and Japan in Cardiff and the Japan vs. Japan game in Shizuoka during the most recent World Cup. Both crucial matches were lost by Ireland, and Sexton was powerless to save them.

More recently, he watched with his son Luca while Ireland's summer series was played out, and he confessed that it was an odd feeling to be sitting there.

He feels that he is still as motivated as ever and that he would still be in that state of mind even if the Lions had not passed on him in the summer.

Before the conclusion of the following Six Nations, Sexton will meet with the IRFU to discuss a contract extension that will send him to France in 2023.

He added of his passion to play, "I think the day that isn't the case I will walk away, 100%, but it's there at the moment."

# Chapter 4: Career Highlights

## Sexton's most memorable matches

Johnny Sexton's extraordinary career has been peppered with milestones, and on Saturday in Nantes, he made rugby history once again.

In the Rugby World Cup victory over Tonga, Ireland was easily defeated, the fly-half passed Ronan O'Gara to surpass him as the nation's all-time leading scorer.

Throughout a 14-year international voyage, the 38-year-old British & Irish Lion has broken records while making field goals from in front of the posts appear simple.

Here, we review ten of the most significant locations that helped to define one of the all-time top 10s in gaming.

## First Game: Leinster 62 - Border Reivers 14, January 2006

As a late replacement in a Celtic League game on a freezing Friday night in Donnybrook, a young Sexton made his professional debut.

Captain Felipe Contepomi was replaced by Sexton in the 75th minute as Leinster defeated Border Reivers behind a hat-trick from Gary Brown.

The 20-year-old was given his club debut by Michael Cheika in front of fewer than 4,000 spectators after a succession of standout performances for St. Mary's College.

**First Trophy: Champions Cup, won in May 2009**

If we exclude the 2002 Leinster Schools Senior Cup, then Sexton's first major trophy and his team's first victory in the competition came in 2009.

Early on in Leinster's semi-final match against Munster, Contepomi suffered an apparent fatal injury, but Sexton came to the rescue.

Following their upset of the defending champions, Sexton and the rising blue tide defeated the Leicester Tigers in a thrilling game in Edinburgh, with the 23-year-old Sexton kicking the game-winning penalty 10 minutes from the end.

## First Ireland Capfor: 2009 Autumn Internationals

After proving his ability to handle big-game situations in the spring, Sexton handled a challenging maiden international assignment at a soggy RDS Arena against a very tough Fijian team.

Sexton kicked seven out of seven goals in the victory (41-6), earning him match-winning honors.

Despite finishing the game with a broken bone in his hand, he kept his spot for South Africa's visit a week later and kicked all 15 points in an exciting five-point triumph over the World champions.

## first Lions Tour: Australia, 2013

Even though Sexton's first Rugby World Cup may not have gone as planned, his first Lions Tour was a huge success.

## Second Lions Tour: New Zealand, 2017

Sexton was in the center of another famous Lions series four years later.

Following his second-half substitution in the first Test, Warren Gatland reinstated Sexton to the starting XV for the second, resulting in the Lions' first victory in New Zealand since 1993.

Despite having a broken wrist and a ruptured ankle tendon, he continued to play until the 72nd minute of the 15-all draw in Auckland, putting his life on the line.

**First Six Nations Grand Slam 2018**

Sexton may have played on Six Nations championship teams in 2014 and 2015, but a Grand Slam was the only honor lacking from his highly sought-after résumé.

Up until 2018, when Ireland stomped to a clean sweep thanks to Sexton's improbable score, which gave them a round one victory in Paris with the clock running out.

Sexton became only the second Irish player to win the World Player of the Year award after Keith Wood won the first prize in 2001 after their victorious tour ended at Twickenham.

## Century Of Caps: Ireland 60–5–Japan, November 2021

In a classy way, Sexton honored his 100th appearance with a try in the second half of Ireland's rout of Japan in Dublin.

Sexton received a standing ovation before the game began for becoming the seventh Irishman, after Brian O'Driscoll, O'Gara, Rory Best, Paul O'Connell, John Hayes, and Cian Healy, to reach a century of appearances.

Similar to what he achieved in 2009, Sexton followed up a significant performance with an even more memorable one, helping Ireland defeat New Zealand 29-20 and reaffirm their place among the top teams in the world.

## In New Zealand, you're on top of the world

Ireland won a series in New Zealand for the first time in 28 years thanks in large part to Sexton, who was at the pinnacle of his craft down under.

He kept his calm throughout the decider in Wellington and reached 1,000 Test points as a result.

With the 33-22 victory, Andy Farrell's team overtook France, which had previously beaten them to the Guinness Six Nations earlier in the year, as the top-ranked team in the world.

## Double delight on home soil

In his home stadium, Ireland's star player said goodbye to the Guinness Six Nations as the tournament's record points scorer and Grand Slam-winning captain.

Sexton passed O'Gara a week after tying him with 557 points in the Championship. It was only natural that Sexton did so against England, the team he first faced in his Six Nations career back in 2010.

Although it was Ireland's third Six Nations Slam overall, it was their first at home since 1948 and will always be associated with Sexton's record-breaking achievements.

## Ireland's number one

And Sexton's try in Ireland's World Cup victory against Tonga further carved his name into Irish rugby lore.

With 1,090 points at the end of the night, he overtook O'Gara to become his nation's top scorer. Only Owen Farrell, Jonny Wilkinson, and Dan Carter are ahead of him on the all-time list.

## His individual awards and accolades

Due to his talent and popularity in Ireland, Johnny Sexton

impact on rugby union for the better part of seventeen years in this nation. He first played for the Leinster province back in 2005.

Soon after, Ireland made its appearance, setting the tone for the majority of the next 20 years. When he was 24 years old, he led his team to a 41-6 victory over Fiji by kicking 777 goals, including five conversions and two penalties.

That marked the start of a successful worldwide career chock full of awards and memorable occasions. The recipient of the 2018 World Rugby Player of the Year award, who scored a drop goal against New Zealand in New Zealand, is shown in the video below. These are just a few instances that best illustrate the magnificence of the Leinster man.

## Ireland Career Awards

Sexton has consistently been there for Irish rugby during its heyday. The Dubliner has contributed significantly to 12 trophy victories, one World Rugby Player of the Year title, and three total nominations.

- 4x Six Nations Championships (2014, 2015, 2018, 2023)
- 2x Grand Slam titles (2018 and 2023)
- 3x Triple Crown three wins (2018, 2022, and 2023)
- 3x Test Series successes (2014, 2018, and 2022)
- 1x Rugby Player of the Year (2018)
- A World Cup victory is the one trophy that eludes him with Ireland.

# Sexton Career Stats and Individual Accolades

The Leinster veteran has been a part of a staggering number of team victories, and his numbers and awards are also quite impressive.

## Longevity

At 37 years and 250 days old, Sexton was already the second-oldest rugby player in Ireland's history when he played against England in March. He is presently only second to John Hayes, who played for Ireland against Scotland in 2011 at the age of 37 years and 277 days.

When Sexton competes at the Rugby World Cup in 2023, he will break the age record for an Irish player.

## Caps

With 113 caps as of the Rugby World Cup in 2023, Sexton is currently ranked fifth in Ireland's all-time appearance list.

More than him, just four athletes have represented the nation:

- Brian O'Driscoll (133)
- O'Gara, Ronan (128)
- Clan Healy (125)
- Rory Best (124)

Paul O'Connell, another candidate for the title of Ireland's greatest player ever, has only received one more cap than Sexton, who has received five. Scrum-half Conor Murray has 107 caps, making him the player with the most active appearances after Sexton.

**Try-Threat from Fly-half**

Sexton has managed to score sixteen tries for his country throughout his career, despite not scoring a try for Ireland since their victory over Japan in the Aviva Stadium back on November 6, 2021.

During a 22-26 loss to France in a pre-2011 Rugby World Cup fixture,

Sexton scored his first try for Ireland. In games where Sexton scored a try, Ireland has won 11 out of 11.

Sexton would get into the top 10 for most tries scored for Ireland if he scores two tries in the 2023 Rugby World Cup.

## Can Overtake O'gara As The Rwc's All-time Points Scorer

Sexton has 1050 points, which places him second on Ireland's all-time points list.

On the all-time Ireland points list, he is thirty-three points behind Ronan O'Gara; therefore, it is possible that at the 2023 Rugby World Cup, he will overtake O'Gara and become Ireland's all-time leading points scorer.

With the help of 15 tries, 165 conversions, 211 penalties, and 4 drop goals for Ireland, Sexton has scored 1050 points overall. While representing Ireland, the fly-half has scored an average of 9.29 points per game.

Ireland, which has more points than all but one of the top 10 scorers, Ollie Campbell averaged 9.86 points per game throughout 22 appearances, totaling 217 points.

Sexton has scored 22 points in a game most times for Ireland. This rank as Ireland's tenth-highest point total in a game came in a 32-18 victory over England in 2021. Top of the list is Ronan O'Gara, who scored 32 points against Samoa in 2003.

**Captain Fantastic**

Sexton has led Ireland 25 times, which puts him behind Rory Best (38) and Brian O'Driscoll (83). Paul O'Connell (28) and Keith Wood (36). Unless there is an injury, Sexton will likely surpass Paul O'Connell on this list at the current Rugby World Cup.

Sexton's 84% win percentage as Ireland's captain is one of the most striking features of his leadership of the Irish team. That is 11% more than William Crawford (1924–1927), his closest rival. It also places Paul O'Connell (64.29%), Rory Best (63.1%), and Brian O'Driscoll (62.65%), three illustrious Irish leaders, far ahead of them.

Of course, Sexton has had the good fortune to captain one of the best Irish players in recent memory. Having said that, his track record speaks volumes about his leadership abilities and what he must have learned from Brian O'Driscoll and Paul O'Connell.

**Club Career**

Leinster has employed Johnny Sexton twice. The first of those lasted from 2006 to 2013. Sexton would later shock everyone by joining Racing 92 in France.

He returned to Leinster in 2015 after an unsuccessful 18-month stay in France that didn't exactly go as planned.

Sexton established himself as an all-time Leinster great during that time by amassing 1646 points over

189 games to become the club's all-time leading scorer.

## Leinster career Accolades

With Leinster, he has also enjoyed tremendous success (although we won't dwell too much on his 18-month stint at Racing 92).

Sexton has received numerous honors with Leinster:

- 4x European Championship Cup(2009, 2011, 2012, and 2018)
- 1x European Challenge Cup (2013)

- 6x Pro 14 (2008, 2013, 2018, 2019, 2020, 2021)
- 2x Irish Shields (2022 and 2023)

## The Best-ever Rugby Player In Ireland?

Is Johnny Sexton the best rugby player Ireland has ever produced? At this point, you would probably have to choose Brian O'Driscoll over Johnny Sexton as Ireland's greatest-ever rugby player, according to the consensus. Legendary Irish forward and captain Paul O'Connell would also have to be mentioned in the discussion of Ireland's greatest-ever player.

While most people rank O'Driscoll as the best, Sexton has a legitimate claim to the crown as well. You'd be insane not to suggest Sexton belongs in that conversation if you looked at the Leinster fly-half's trophy haul at the club and international levels, looked at the records, and saw the performances. It also comes from a

A man from Munster who still favors Ronan O'Gara nowadays.

The significant caveat, in my opinion, with Sexton's achievement is that he represented Leinster and Ireland during a heyday for Irish rugby.

You could argue that his success with the national team was made simpler by the talented players he was surrounded with.

**World cup glory can make Sexton Ireland's greatest**

The tone of the discussion will drastically shift if Ireland can disprove me and many other skeptics by shocking the world and winning their first-ever Rugby World Cup.

In my opinion, Johnny Sexton can only be referred to as "Ireland's Greatest Ever Rugby Player" after that has occurred.

There you have it, then. Is Johnny Sexton the best rugby player Ireland has ever produced? No, not just now, but he may still lay claim to that dist inction.

If Sexton guides Ireland to Rugby World Cup success, many will consider him to be Ireland's greatest player in history.

## His impact on the game of rugby

Rugby has been significantly impacted by Johnny Sexton, both with Leinster and Ireland. He is among the greatest players of all time in terms of success and impact.

Sexton is a fly-half of the finest caliber, possessing all the qualities necessary for success at the highest level. He is a talented playmaker with sharp passing instincts. He can carry the ball well and kick the ball consistently. Sexton is an excellent motivator and leader. He can motivate and motivate his team members.

Sexton has contributed to Leinster's success in several competitions, including four Heineken Cups and five Pro12 championships. In addition, he has guided Ireland to several victories, including three Six

Nations titles and a triumph over the All Blacks.

Sexton's influence on rugby extends beyond only his performance on the field. He serves as an example for young athletes everywhere. He demonstrates that anything is feasible with effort, commitment, and resolve.

The following are some of the ways Johnny Sexton has influenced rugby:

- He has improved the level of competition at the fly-half position.
- A new generation of rugby players are motivated by him.

- He has contributed to the growth in popularity and accessibility of rugby.
- He has demonstrated that it is possible to be a successful rugby player, a role model, and a decent human being all at the same time.

Sexton is a true hero and is destined to become one of the all-time great rugby players.

# Chapter 5: Beyond Rugby

## Sexton's life outside of rugby

Behind every successful rugby player comes a great woman.

Laura was the subject of the initial Jonathan Sexton dating rumors. For the majority of their followers, both started dating in 2005.

Sexton made the daring decision to marry his childhood girlfriend in the year 2004. In 2013, Jonathan and Laura exchanged vows at the 13th-century Holy Trinity Church in Adare, Ireland.

The pair is father to five children: Luca, Amy, Sophie, Chase, and Katerina Sexton.

Laura Sexton, a teacher, has a propensity to do things practically and offers unwavering support to her husband and her gorgeous children.

Once you get to know him, you'll see that he's a quiet, shy person who occasionally speaks so softly that you can hardly hear him.

Deep down, Johnny is also a really real, sensitive person. The recognition and admiration he has received throughout the years do not diminish his ability as a sportsman.

Years ago, Johnny Sexton used to often reassure his family that he would wear the Irish green shirt because he felt complete assurance sometimes on flimsy grounds. There was always "a little bit of the devil in him" according to some family members.

The father of Jonathan Sexton was a former rugby player who, through two of his kids (Jerry and Johnny), continued to pursue his goals of playing the sport after retiring.

Clare Sexton, the mother of Jonathan Sexton, works as a housekeeper and a hairdresser at the well-known Rathgar Hair Salon in the southern part of the city. She also helps Brenda Sexton, the grandmother of her son's father, with apparel sales.

Jerry, Mark, and Gillian Sexton are the names of Johnny's three siblings. Jerry was one of Johnny's groomsmen, and Mark served as his best man.

Jeremiah aka Jerry Sexton, Johnny's younger brother, currently plays professional rugby union for the Southern Kings of South Africa (born

20 January 1993). Like his brother, he played for Leinster Rugby while still in high school.

Mark and Gillian both actively avoid the public, leading quiet lives, in contrast to Jerry.

Making a distinction between living a pleasant lifestyle and being realistic on the field is not a difficult decision.

Being the highest earner in Ireland Rugby means having a lot of money to live a normal life, with a season salary of €650,000 (as of the writing of this).

Johnny Sexton doesn't offer much of a refreshing counterpoint to the present rugby world of flashy cars, enormous homes, and social media since he leads a lavish lifestyle.

Johnny has continued to live in terror of retiring early after seeing what happened to Jamie Heaslip, a former Irish rugby union player who represented Leinster and Ireland.

Johnny Sexton constantly worries about getting hurt and having to leave the game early.

He believes that every rugby player, including himself, is just one injury away from being rendered permanently unable to play the sport. His words are;

"With other players, I've observed that. Jamie Heaslip played an amazing number of games before being suspended due to one incident. Just one bad bag tackle, not even during a match, but rather during practice. The biggest worry I have is thinking about this.

When they have money, very few successful athletes would say no to continuing their schooling. Johnny Sexton, however, is not one of them.

He earned a Bachelor of Commerce from University College Dublin.

Johnny Sexton practices his religion and believes in God. He grew up in a Catholic household. His grandmother and grandfather forced him to go to catholic mass with his parents in Dublin when he was a little child.

# Chapter 6: Legacy

## Sexton's impact on Irish rugby

Irish rugby has been significantly impacted by Johnny Sexton. He is among the greatest players of all time in terms of success and impact.

In 2009, Sexton made his international debut for Ireland, and he rapidly became the team's go-to fly-half. Since then, he has accrued the most caps for Ireland and received multiple individual honors, including World Rugby Player of the Year in 2018.

Ireland has won several games under Sexton's direction, including three Six Nations titles and a triumph over the All Blacks. With more than 1,000 points scored, he is also Ireland's all-time leading scorer.

Sexton's influence on Irish rugby extends beyond only his performance on the field. He serves as an example for young athletes everywhere. He demonstrates that anything is feasible with effort, commitment, and resolve.

The following are some of the ways Johnny Sexton has influenced Irish rugby:

- He has improved the level of play in Ireland in the fly-half position.
- A new generation of Irish rugby players is motivated by him.
- He has contributed to the success of the Irish national team.
- He has demonstrated that it is possible to be an admirable role model and a successful international rugby player.

Although Sexton hasn't competed since March, when he was a crucial component of the Irish team's Grand Slam victory, the 38-year-old is still leading the Irish lineup.

Given the prolonged absence, some people might be tempted to take it easy, but not Sexton, who, according to Ringrose, has been a crucial component of Ireland's preparations.

## High Standard

For someone who has worked there for such a long time, "he operates at a level that demands (a high standard)," the speaker claimed.

You can probably see it in some of the greatest athletes from different sports; they all have that competitive edge that brings out the best in you.

James Lowe, a wing, claims that Sexton is not a case of "doing as I say, not as I do," since the fly-half also has high expectations for himself.

"He expects the same things of himself as he does of us. That he has persevered this long and performed at such a high level is a testament to him, according to Lowe.

But I don't want to compliment him excessively!

"The group benefits from having a strong emotional leader who is also a rugby player."

We're all rowing in the same direction in the same boat, so having a man like that at the helm means a lot to the team.

"If I had to play with him, I would choose to do so," you said.

## Coaching excellence

Along with the brilliance on the field, the club has a lot of quality off it thanks to head coach Andy Farrell's stellar backroom staff.

"The coaching staff as a whole, in my opinion, gets along nicely. Everyone in this setting wants what's best for one another, said Lowe.

Along with the aforementioned, Sexton has positively influenced Irish rugby culture. He is renowned for his zeal, diligence, and leadership. He has encouraged the Irish people to support the team and helped the Irish team develop a winning mentality.

People of all ages in Ireland look up to Sexton, who is revered as a national figure. He serves as an inspiration for young people all over the world and demonstrates that anything is achievable with effort, commitment, and resolve.

## His status as one of the greatest rugby players of all time

**An unrivaled legacy**

There is little one can do but step aside and watch the extraordinary triumph accomplished by the man who must now be regarded as this island's greatest rugby player ever as the sun begins to set on Johnny Sexton's illustrious career.

Sexton's career has generated more than any other player before him, packing a lifetime's worth of memorable moments into a flawless 17-year span, from the drop goal in

Paris to that second-half performance in Cardiff.

Sexton has consistently delivered in crucial situations, regardless of the jersey, whether it is the red of the Lions, the green of Ireland, the blue of Leinster, or briefly the blue of Racing Metro (let's try to act like that never happened).

Johnny Sexton's rivals for the crown
Since that infamous May day in 2009, when Leinster wrested the title of Ireland's finest player from Munster as well as ROG, the former St. Mary's College student has come a long way.

The Leinster fly-half produced one of Irish sport's most iconic images as he loomed over the player who had just drop-kicked Ireland to unbelievable Grand Slam glory a few months earlier. This moment also symbolized the mindset of a player who would push Irish rugby to previously unimaginable heights.

Sexton's magnetic affinity with accumulating medals has seen him elevate to the argument of whether or not he is Ireland's best player, putting to bed the boring discussion of who was Ireland's greatest fly-half.

Of course, Brian O'Driscoll, a former teammate of his from Leinster and Ireland, will be his major rival. But Sexton now stands atop the Irish rugby kingdom after significantly outpacing his predecessor's trophy total and winning the one last honor that always eluded O'Driscoll: the World Rugby Player of the Year title.

Stuart Barnes famously christened O'Driscoll, saying, "They call him God, but I reckon he's a better player than that." For Sexton to surpass nearly every mark set by the center in fewer tests only serves to highlight the extent of Sexton's brilliance, which we have been so fortunate to witness.

## The ideal big-game hunter

The fly-half of Leinster follows in the titanic footprints of the extraordinary Felipe Contepomi. The RDS crowd admired the erratic Argentine, but as he left for the Cote d'Azur, his absence was barely noticed as Sexton led the 2009 Heineken Cup champions to back-to-back victories in 2011 and 2012.

The 2011 final in particular is one of the most breath-taking displays in Irish sport, not just rugby, as Sexton led an Istanbul-like comeback from a 22-6 deficit to help Leinster win.

Few could imagine a more fitting setting for Sexton's brilliant second-half performance that day than the stadium that has become synonymous with Irish rugby legend, from Munster's moving European victories to Rog's aforementioned ending of 61 years of Irish agony.

The fly-half summoned the courage and confidence deep within Principality Stadium to rally his Leinster colleagues despite being 16 points behind at the half.

The fact that Sexton went on to score all of Leinster's points on the day, except a single Nathan Hines try, made what happened in that second half all the more fascinating. Brian O'Driscoll recalled his fly half's fervent sermon after his team's triumphant celebrations, adding that "He speaks when the time needs it but I think he really stood up to the plate this time around and was there to be a senior player as a ten." He had to be a senior player and a leader today, and he was both."

The less said about Sexton's two-year sabbatical in the affluent Paris suburbs, during which time Leinster struggled without their favorite son, the better. The fly-half guided Racing to consecutive Top 14 play-off appearances during his time there, but both times they fell short against eventual champions Toulon and Stade Francais.

Following Sexton's departure, Leinster's potential rugby dynasty in Europe came to an end, as the province lost in the final rounds to a Toulon team that accomplished the extraordinary accomplishment of winning three consecutive European Cups.

Thankfully, a compromise between Sexton and the IRFU led to the fly half's return to these shores before the 2015–16 season. Since then, Sexton and Leinster have been virtually unstoppable forces at home, winning a record four straight league titles and earning a fourth European star for their jerseys.

**Taking Up Ireland's Call**

However, it is not just Sexton's accomplishments for Leinster that have propelled him to the top of the sport; the former World Player of the Year has also earned 113 caps for Ireland.

Sexton has played a key role in delivering Ireland a record four Six Nations titles over the previous decade, with two of these victories also finishing in the hallowed form of Grand Slams. Sexton is the driving force behind Ireland's most trophy-laden period in the history of the sport.

When trying to describe the pure brilliance of Ireland's record points scorer, there are a plethora of crucial moments to pick from, much like his Leinster career. One finds it difficult to forget the first weekend of the 2018 Six Nations competition when Sexton surprised the Stade de France by making an absurd 45-meter drop goal in the game's closing play.

But like many great athletes, Sexton's desire to compete has grown to such a degree that, as he approaches his 38th birthday, it seems to be the only thing that can keep him going.

A prime example is Sexton's leadership of Andy Farrell's team during last summer's historic series victory over the All Blacks, one of Irish sport's most notable accomplishments. Ireland had never defeated the world's most dominant rugby power until a little over six years prior.

Now, in 2023, with four test victories under our belt—all of which Sexton started—we are on the verge of our period of rugby dominance.

There was nothing more fitting for Sexton to do on Saturday night when the Aviva Stadium celebrated its beloved conductor one last time than to do so while carrying a Grand Slam after one final victory over the old foe.

The Leinster fly half's trophy collection is suddenly overflowing. Nevertheless, space can undoubtedly be created for the most sought of them all, with Sexton preparing to captain his nation to the World Cup this fall to end the historic quarter final curse.

The best rugby player from Ireland will now be regarded as its greatest sportsperson if the two-time Slam champion and his Ireland squad are successful in capturing the Webb Ellis Cup.

A perfect conclusion to a fairy tale career. Sexton has led both club and nation from perennial underachievers to standard bearers everywhere from Dublin to Chicago to Wellington and everywhere in between, and for this, he will never be forgotten.

# His future plans

Johnny Sexton, the captain of Ireland's rugby team, is preparing for his financial future after his company invested more than €550,00 in a directors' pension fund last year.

According to Sexton's JAS Management & Promotions Ltd.'s financial statements, directors' compensation climbed more than seven times in the 12 months leading up to the end of September of last year, from €82,859 to €653,002.

However, after making no pension payments the year before, the biggest portion of the directors' compensation was €552,509.

The increase in directors' compensation helped the company register a loss of €460,556 last year, down from a post-tax profit of €362,189 the year before, a difference of €822,745.

The company's cumulative profits at the end of September 2022 were €2.33 million due to the loss from the previous year.

Following the pension payout, the company's cash funds decreased by €493,675 from €1.94 million to €1.44 million.

During the year, the firm's financial assets' value decreased somewhat, falling from €757,455 to €729,513.

The announcement of the pension payment from the company comes just perhaps a few months before Sexton announces his retirement from the professional game following the conclusion of the Rugby World Cup in France this year.

Irish supporters will be hoping that the retirement postpones the October 28th final in Paris.

Sexton's lucrative last 18-month playing deal with the IRFU will expire upon his retirement from the sport.

Sexton's job is listed as "sportsman or related work" on JAS Management & Promotions' annual return, and earlier this year, Sexton, who turned 38 last month, said he intends to pursue a career in business after retiring from the game.

I've been doing some work experience there for the past few years, one day a week, so I'll enter that and see how it goes, he added.

Sexton's off-field business transactions are currently being managed by Conor Ridge's Horizon Sports, whose other well-known clients include Open champion Shane Lowry and Munster and Ireland's Peter O'Mahony.

From a playing and business standpoint, the Dubliner is the most successful Irish player currently, but he still has a ways to go before he can match the success of his retired Leinster and Ireland teammate Brian O'Driscoll, whose main company had accumulated profits of €9.66 million at the end of last August.

Sexton, who is presently suspended but is scheduled to play again for Ireland in the opening World Cup match, has 113 caps for Ireland and 1,050 points.

In January 2020, Andy Farrell named the former World Rugby Player of the Year as the captain of Ireland.

One of Irish Rugby's most accomplished players, Sexton earlier this year guided Ireland to a Grand Slam.

One of several rugby players with management businesses to handle income from business endeavors like sponsorships and image rights is Sexton, who founded his company in 2010.